FORT PULASKI AND THE DEFENSE OF SAVANNAH

CIVIL WAR SERIES

TEXT BY HERBERT M. SCHILLER

Maps by George Skoch

Thanks to Kent Cave and Tally Kirkland at Fort Pulaski National Monument
and to Daniel Brown at Fort McAllister State Historical Park.

Published by Eastern National, copyright 1997.

Eastern National provides quality educational products and services to
America's national parks and other public trusts.

Cover: National Park Service photograph of Ft. Pulaski National Monument.

Back cover: Original map from General Gillmore's report on the siege of Fort Pulaski from the National Archives.

Printed on recycled paper.

FORT PULASKI AND THE DEFENSE OF SAVANNAH

*O*riginating on the slopes of the Appalachian Mountains, the Savannah River flows east, forming the boundary between South Carolina and Georgia. Twelve miles from the coast it passes Savannah, joined by hundreds of interconnecting channels twisting their way into the sea. Among the channels are hundreds of tidal islands. They are covered with grass and reeds and resemble a savannah at low tide. Closest to the ocean is a deposit of mud lying between the two channels of the Savannah River; it is Cockspur Island and the home of Fort Pulaski.

Fort Pulaski was part of the defense of Savannah, the most strategic point along the Georgia coast. The expanding international cotton industry made Savannah a major international port in the pre–Civil War South. Three railroads converged on the city. Shipbuilding, marine industries, and railroad shops were the primary military industries.

Forts such as Pulaski had two missions—to prevent the passage of ships and to resist attack. Stopping ships required the proper number and caliber of guns. Ground defense required inaccessibility and distance from bombarding artillery. Fort Pulaski was ready for both missions. Before the Civil War, the chief engineer of the United States Army had said, "You might as well bombard the Rocky Mountains as Fort Pulaski. . . . The fort could not be reduced in a month's firing with any number of guns of manageable caliber."

Cockspur Island had been the site of forts since pre–Revolutionary War days. First was Fort George in 1761, a palisaded log blockhouse dismantled and abandoned by patriot forces in 1776 because it was indefensible against the British fleet.

Fort Greene, named for the Revolutionary War patriot Nathanael Greene, who is buried on nearby Mulberry Grove Plantation, was built in 1794–95. In 1804 a hurricane swept Cockspur, destroying the fort and drowning part of the garrison. The island remained unused until the 1820s.

Fort Pulaski was part of a coastal defensive system begun after the War of 1812 that stretched from Maine to Louisiana. Although Cockspur was chosen as a site in the early 1820s, construction did not begin until 1829. The original plans called for a structure identical to Fort Sumter—a two-story pentagonal fort with three tiers of guns. Engineers determined that Cockspur's muddy composition would not support such a weight of masonry. The plan was modified to a single story, one row of casemate guns, and above, a row of parapet (barbette) guns.

Construction was initially supervised by Major Samuel Babcock. In the autumn of 1829 Lieutenant Robert E. Lee, newly graduated from the United States Military Academy, arrived as Babcock's assistant. Ill health prevented Babcock from taking an active role and it fell to Lee to locate the site of the fort and to begin the construction of the drainage canals and dikes.

Assigned to Virginia in 1831, Lee would not visit the fort again until the Civil War. In 1833 the partially completed fort was named for Count Casimir Pulaski, who had been mortally wounded in 1779 in the battle of Savannah. Malaria, yellow fever, typhoid, and dysentery halted work each summer. Work continued, largely under the direction of Lieutenant Joseph K. F. Mansfield, and the fort was completed in 1847.

Twenty-five million bricks were used to build the fort; most were made on nearby plantations. Granite and sandstone were brought from New York and Connecticut. The Corps of Engineers rented slaves from neighboring plantations for hard labor; masons and carpenters came from Savannah and the North. Twenty 32-pounder naval guns were installed in 1840. Although the fort was designed for 150 guns, not a single gun was added until after it was seized by Georgia authorities in 1861.

Fort Pulaski has five sides, called faces. Two guard the south channel of the Savannah River; two, the north channel. The gorge, the least vulnerable side of the fort, faces west toward Savannah. The three ocean-facing angles of the fort each had a short face, the *pan coupé*, at the angle of the walls. Each *pan coupé* has a

Principal transporta-
tion routes and
defenses of
Savannah.
Fort Pulaski protect-
ed this important
commercial center
from seaborne
attack. The fall of
Pulaski greatly
strengthened the
Federal blockade
of Southern ports.

Plan of Fort Pulaski

George Skoch

South
Carolina
passed her
Ordinance of
Secession on
December 20,
1860; the
news was
greeted in
Savannah
with celebra-
tion and
demonstra-
tions of
support.

single casemate and embrasure (opening) for a gun to protect the potential blind spot at the angle. All the walls of the fort are seven and a half feet thick and rise twenty-five feet above the water-filled moat. The gorge is protected by the triangular demilune, which has been remodeled and differs today from the original design. The entire structure is surrounded by a moat, 48 feet wide around the fort and 32 feet wide along the demilune.

South Carolina passed her Ordinance of Secession on December 20, 1860; the news was greeted in Savannah with celebration and demonstrations of support. Six nights later, the militia and torch-bearing citizens marched through the city. That same night Major Robert Anderson's Federal troops slipped from Fort Moultrie on Sullivan Island into Fort Sumter in Charleston Harbor. Outraged Georgians protested in Savannah; the mob called for the siezure of Fort Pulaski before it, too, could be used to block the river and access to the port of Savannah. On January 1, 1861, Governor Joseph E.

Brown met with Colonel Alexander R. Lawton, commander of the 1st Volunteer Regiment of Georgia, along with various regimental officers, to plan the seizure of Fort Pulaski. Meetings continued the next day. Early on January 3, details of infantrymen and artillerymen, accompanied by six small artillery pieces, marched to the waterfront in the rain, amid cheering crowds. There, they boarded the comandeered United States sidewheel steamer *Ida* and descended to Cockspur. Landing at the north wharf, the Georgians marched into the fort, then under the care of an ordnance sergeant who surrendered the fort, its rusting guns, and a small supply of powder and ammunition. Taking possession of the fort, Colonel Lawton raised the Georgia flag over the ramparts. On January 16, 1861, the Georgia state convention met to consider the state's course; they voted to withdraw from the Union and passed Articles of Secession.

Fort Pulaski had been neglected badly over the years. The quarters were unfit to live in; the overgrown parade was

unusable; a morass of silt and marsh grass filled the moat. Even with the labor of 125 slaves, the Georgians spent months restoring the fort to livable and defensible condition. The men strung a telegraph wire between the fort and Savannah.

During the first half of the year, the 1st Regiment of Georgia Volunteers, along with other state troops, prepared Fort Pulaski and a network of defenses on neighboring islands and waterways. These defenses stretched from earthen Fort McAllister on the Great Ogeechee River into South Carolina to the north.

In October 1861, Major Charles H. Olmstead took command of Fort Pulaski; he would shortly be promoted to colonel. A native of Savannah, he had been educated at the Georgia Military Academy in Marietta and was a businessman as well as regimental adjutant when Georgia seceded.

During 1861 two lines of coastal defenses were developed in Georgia. A series of batteries and forts were erected on the outer, "barrier," islands, and a series of additional defenses were constructed further inland along major waterways. With the fall of Hilton Head Island in November 1861, the outer line was subsequently abandoned.

During 1861 and the first six weeks of 1862, thousands of pounds of gunpowder and ammunition were brought to the fort. In addition, Olmstead was able to boost his artillery complement to 48 guns, including 12-inch mortars, two English Blakely rifles, and 10-inch columbiads.

The *Ida* continued to visit the fort daily, bringing such supplies as she could carry. Most of the arms, lumber, food, and gunpowder was brought on barges towed by other steamers.

On February 21, 1861, Captain Josiah Tattnall, a native of Savannah, resigned from the United States Navy and became the flag officer of the Georgia navy. Tattnall's force consisted of five small, armed steamers—the *Savannah*, his flagship, and the *Sampson, Lady Davis, Resolute*, and *Huntress*. They patrolled the intercoastal waterway and other shallow channels between the various marshy islands, reassuring residents who feared Federal raids. The vessels also towed supply barges and delivered stores to Fort Pulaski.

On May 27, 1861, the first Federal blockading vessel arrived in Tybee Roads at the mouth of the Savannah River. The port was now "closed," although a few more blockade runners were able to dash in during the subsequent months. After

THEODORE DAVIS MADE THIS DRAWING OF THE FORT IN MAY 1861.

(AMERICAN HERITAGE PRINT COLLECTION)

THIS PHOTOGRAPH TAKEN AFTER THE BOMBARDMENT OF THE FORT SHOWS A CONFEDERATE COLUMBIAD AND A MORTAR.

(LC)

additional blockaders arrived, members of the 1st Volunteer Regiment on Tybee Island, southeast of Cockspur Island, erected a sand fort near the lighthouse, which was at the northeastern end of the island. The armed fort kept the blockaders at a distance and discouraged landings by Federal forces. During the autumn of 1861, rumors reached the Confederates that Union forces were assembling for an invasion of the South Atlantic coast.

In early November General Robert E. Lee was appointed commander of the newly consolidated Confederate Department of South Carolina, Georgia, and East Florida. He arrived in South Carolina on November 7, 1861, the day that Port Royal Sound fell to a Federal army-navy combined expedition. Lee immediately ordered Confederates to abandon Hilton Head and Saint Phillip's Islands bordering the sound. He then began to organize his new plan. He would abandon exposed Georgia defenses at Darien, Brunswick, and on the Saint Marys River and had the artillery and troops sent to Savannah. Lee planned to guard the coast with cavalry and use the Savannah, Albany and Gulf Railroad to move troops from Savannah south to any threatened points along the coast.

The Federal success on the South Carolina coast was the culmination of War Department plans hatched five months earlier. Union strategy called for blockading Confederate ports.

BRIGADIER GENERAL
THOMAS W. SHERMAN

(USAMHI)

BRIGADIER GENERAL QUINCY A. GILLMORE

(USAMHI)

Port Royal Sound, South Carolina, and Fernandina, Florida, were selected as coaling stations to sustain Federal ships in Southern waters. Commodore Samuel F. Du Pont and Brigadier General Thomas W. Sherman led the joint expedition. After the naval bombardment drove away the defenders, infantrymen quickly occupied Hilton Head Island. Sherman, a native Rhode Islander, was a United States Military Academy graduate and had served as an artillery officer. He commanded three brigades and three attached regiments. Among Sherman's staff officers was chief engineer Captain Quincy A. Gillmore, ordnance officer Lieutenant Horace Porter, and chief topographical engineer Lieutenant James H. Wilson. All would have full careers during the subsequent four years.

Sherman quickly occupied adjacent South Carolina Islands and secured the harbors of Port Royal and Saint Helena. The day after Confederates abandoned

Hilton Head Island, the Georgia troops removed their guns from the sand fort on Tybee Island and withdrew. Sherman and Gillmore did not land on Tybee Island until November 25. They went to the northeast shore and, from over a mile away, examined Fort Pulaski through telescopes. Both men believed that they could reduce the fort from Tybee using a combination of mortars and breaching guns, the conventional armament for such a task. Within a week, Gillmore ordered twenty mortars, eight heavy rifled guns, and eight columbiads.

Conventional military doctrine called for plunging mortar fire to penetrate and disrupt the parapets and destroy the underlying casemate arches while the smoothbore columbiads slowly shattered the brick wall. Rifled guns were a new development, and few military experiments deploying them against masonry fortifications had been published. Rifled guns were reported to be more effective than smoothbore guns of comparable caliber when fired from distances of a mile away. Gillmore was familiar with these European reports and chose to add a few rifled guns to his requested armament as an experiment. Although General Sherman had little enthusiasm for the rifled guns (he believed that the mortars and columbiads could eventually reduce the fort), he consented to Gillmore's experiment.

In early December, Colonel Rudolph Rosa's 46th New York Infantry occupied Tybee Island. They were soon joined by members of the 3d Rhode Island Heavy Artillery, who mounted guns in the abandoned Confederate sand fort at the northeastern end of the island. The 7th Connecticut, commanded by Colonel

Alfred H. Terry, joined the New Yorkers in late December.

On the afternoon of December 29, the newly promoted Colonel Olmstead was working with a casemated 32-pounder. Three Federals walked out on Kings Point and, standing on the ruins of a burned house, made "defiant and indecent gestures toward the fort." Olmstead later recalled that he wanted to get the elevation "of our 32 Pounders for that particular spot, and accordingly had one of the guns trained upon the group, but without the slightest thought that there would be anything more than a scare for the men. But the shot hit the middle man and probably tore him to pieces. Through my glasses I could see the two others crawling up to the body on hands and knees, and then getting up and running away as fast as their legs could take them; its probability of its being made again with a smooth bore gun at that distance, (a few yards short of a mile), is infinitesimally small."

Olmstead did not know, but he had cut in half a private in the 46th New York. The event made a big impression on the New Yorkers, many of whom were still talking about it a month later. Rumor among the Federals on Tybee Island was that because of the incident,

GOVERNOR JOSEPH E. BROWN OF GEORGIA

(HARPER'S WEEKLY)

COLONEL CHARLES H. OLMSTEAD

(NPS)

Olmstead had been promoted to colonel. Olmstead had actually received his new rank on December 26, three days before the incident.

As Federal forces continued to strengthen their grip on the coastal islands, Lee persevered in strengthening the inner coastal defenses of his department. He visited Fort Pulaski in January 1862, accompanied by Governor Brown, Brigadier General Lawton, and a dozen other army and naval officers. After touring the fort and viewing Olmstead's preparations, he told the colonel, "They will make it very warm for you with shells from that point [Goat Point and Kings Landing on western Tybee Island] but they cannot breach your walls at that distance." Lee knew that the greatest distance that balls could be effective against masonry walls was 800 yards and Tybee Island was over 1,700 yards away. Lee, perhaps unaware of experiments with the new rifled guns, was wrong.

During his visit, Lee directed Olmstead to build sandbag traverses between the barbette guns to protect gunners from bursting shells, to dig ditches on the parade ground to trap rolling shells, and to tear down the wooden structures along the officers' quarters.

Lee further told Olmstead to erect blindage around the entire interior circuit of the fort to cover the casemate doors and to cover the blindage along the gorge with several feet of earth. After Lee's visit, Confederates floated rafts of timber for the blindage down the river into the south channel and up the small irrigation canal into the moat.

In Wall's Cut, a short channel joining the New and Wright Rivers in South Carolina, both rivers roughly parallel to the Savannah River, Confederates had driven pilings and sunk a hulk to obstruct passage to Federal shallow-draft vessels from Port Royal Sound. In mid-January Union soldiers removed the pilings and secured the now-drifting hulk to one side of the channel. Although Sherman and Du Pont initially planned a joint expedition to bypass Fort Pulaski and take the city of Savannah at the end of January, they called it off when naval officers objected that the channels north of the Savannah were too shallow.

Sherman, in the meantime, had ordered Gillmore to examine Jones Island for a possible battery site. Gillmore located a point of dry ground on the Savannah River side of the island, an area that was but a few inches above water at high tide. The battery site was 1,300 yards across the island from the closest wharf site on the north shore.

Jones Island was a gelatinous mixture of mud and grass roots. Gillmore described it:

The substratum being a semi-fluid mud, which is agitated like jelly by the falling of even small bodies upon it, like the jumping of men, or the ramming of earth. . . . Men walking over it are partially sustained by the roots of the reeds and grass and sink in only five or six inches. When

CONFEDERATE CREWS PLACED OBSTRUCTIONS IN THE SAVANNAH RIVER TO BLOCK FEDERAL VESSELS.

(FMTW)

this top support gives way or is broken through they go down two or two and one-half feet and in some places much farther.

In preparation for building the wharf and walkway across the island, soldiers on Daufuskie Island cut 10,000 pine trees during the first four days of February. Rafts of poles, along with sandbags, were brought to Jones Island and a wharf was completed on February 8. A corduroy pathway across the island enabled the infantrymen to carry sandbags and planking for a battery site across the island; they completed their work during the night of February 10. The next two nights, during a winter rainstorm, Federals began to move six cannon across the semifluid island and to the battery platform. Teams of 35 men were responsible for moving two guns at a time, guns that weighed more than two tons apiece. First, three pairs of planks fifteen feet long, one foot wide, and three inches thick were placed in tandem. The first gun was rolled to the end of the first pair. The second gun was rolled onto the second pair. Then the last pair was taken up and pulled into position in front of the first gun. The men sunk to their knees at every step. They were soon unable to hold the slippery, slimy planks and had to attach ropes to drag them forward. Gillmore ordered the men to cease their efforts about 2:00 A.M. and to resume the following night.

The same officers, with new teams of men, resumed their efforts the next night.

The wet, cold infantrymen repeated the procedure again and again until the guns reached the battery platform. The slippery mud offered poor traction for the wheels; frequently a gun would slip off the plank and immediately sink to the axle. The men would carefully lever it back onto the track and begin anew. Guns sliding off the track frequently hit the poles and flipped them up, slamming the men into the mud.

Despite the hardship, the six guns were in the battery before sunrise on February 12. The site was named Battery

Vulcan; the tide lapped within eight inches of the platform. The following day Federal soldiers saw a column of smoke across the waving marsh grass. The unsuspecting *Ida* came steaming down the Savannah River on a regular visit to Fort Pulaski. Battery Vulcan opened on her; five of the six guns recoiled into the ooze and the *Ida* continued unharmed to Fort Pulaski; she later returned to Savannah by way of Lazaretto Creek. The soldiers remounted Vulcan's guns and enlarged the platform.

On February 20, the Union forces erected another six-gun battery, Battery Hamilton, on the western tip of Bird Island, across the north channel of the

SAVANNAH, GEORGIA, PHOTOGRAPHED IN 1865 SHORTLY AFTER THE WAR.

(LC)

Savannah River from Battery Vulcan. Two days later they sank a hulk near Decent Island in Lazaretto Creek, closing all possible routes of resupply to Fort Pulaski. Except for an occasional courier delivering mail and newspapers, the fort was cut off. By this time Fort Pulaski had 48 guns, 45 in the fort and 3 mortars in outside batteries facing Tybee Island.

Before Tybee Island's occupation, one Union observer described it as an outer strip of sand dunes, covered with bushes and low trees, encompassing salt marshes. "The uplands [are] covered with stunted growth of live oak, long-leaved pine, cedar and an occasional palmetto. The marshy strips are clothed in grasses, reeds, [and] strange looking willows." Many of the sand

hills were up to twenty feet high.

On Tybee's east and north shores there were several areas of higher ground; the siege batteries would be constructed on the north shore. The distance from the landing site on the northeast end of the island to the future battery sites was two and a half miles. The last mile was low and marshy and would be crossed by a road corduroyed with brushwood and bundes of sticks in full view of the fort's guns.

By late February Tybee Island was occupied by the 46th New York, the 7th Connecticut, two companies of the 1st New York Volunteer Engineers, five companies of the 8th Maine, two companies of the 3d Rhode Island Heavy Artillery, and a few members of Lieutenant Wilson's company of engineers. On February 21 the first piece of the Tybee Island siege artillery arrived. Captain Gillmore would direct all of the engineer operations for the preparation of the bombardment of Fort Pulaski. The commander of the New York Engineers, however, was a colonel. Gillmore was able to persuade his commander, Brigadier General Sherman, to appoint him as acting (brevet) brigadier general in the interest of an appropriate command structure. Needless to say, Gillmore politicked actively for the appointment behind the scenes.

Over the next seven weeks, thirty-six guns arrived: twelve 13-inch mortars, four 10-inch mortars, six 10-inch columbiads, four 8-inch columbiads, five James rifles of varying calibers, and five 30-pounder Parrott guns. The tube of the 13-inch mortar weighed 17,000 pounds; the tube of the 10-inch columbiad weighed 15,000 pounds. Wharf facilities for unloading the cannon tubes and carriages did not exist on Tybee Island.

The James rifle had been developed by Rhode Island militia general Charles T. James. Its distinctive cone-shaped projectile consisted of a cast iron body and a cage of slanted iron ribs that started near the middle and extended to a solid ring at the lower end. The core of the

WITH WEAPONS LIKE THIS 13-INCH MORTAR, THE FEDERALS HOPED TO PUMMEL FORT PULASKI TO OBLIVION.

(USAMHI)

lower half was hollow and the spaces between each of the eight ribs communicated with the central core at their lower ends. The ribbed lower half of the projectile was encased with soft lead and covered with tin and a greased, sewn canvas jacket. When the gun was fired, the expanding gasses entered the open center of the cage and swelled through the openings between the ribs, forcing the soft lead and tin into the grooves that the greased canvas served to lubricate. The eight elongated ribs and openings resembled a wheel hub and Confederates in the fort would later refer to these projectiles as "cartwheels." James projectiles were generally double the weight of the similar smoothbore caliber roundshot; for example, a 42-pounder James projectile weighed 84 pounds.

The Parrott gun had been developed by Robert P. Parrott, supervisor of the West Point Foundry. He developed a manufacturing process for cast iron rifled cannon

shortly before the Civil War. The tube was rotated horizontally after casting and was water-cooled from the inside, which allowed its more slowly cooling exterior to compress and strengthen the interior. While the hot tube rotated, a wrought iron band was slipped over the breech and, because the tube was rotating, it cooled and clamped itself uniformly providing reinforcing strength. Projectiles for the Parrott gun had a soft metal plate at their base to take the rifling when fired.

Since there was no wharf for getting the guns ashore at Tybee Island, an individual tube or gun carriage was loaded into a lighter on which a platform had been prepared by laying thick planks across the gunwales. The Atlantic beach of Tybee was "remarkable for its heavy surf." At high tide, the soldiers ashore pulled the lighter toward the shore with ropes. Others, sometimes 50 men, would tip the lighters and roll the gun tube into the water. At low tide, up to 250 men would pull on ropes fastened to the tube or carriage and drag it

above the high tide line, a labor that could take more than two hours.

The infantrymen then prepared a sling cart to move the guns inland. First, the gun tube or metal carriage would be placed on a pair of skids made of a pair of twenty-foot long foot-square timbers

A WARTIME SKETCH OF TYBEE ISLAND SHOWING THE MARTELLO TOWER AND LIGHTHOUSE.

(BL)

braced together by three cross pieces. The men then elevated one end of the pair onto the axle of a pair of heavy wheels. They then pulled the gun tube to the middle of the skids. Finally, they elevated the other end of the pair onto another pair of wheels and the sling cart was ready.

The eleven battery sites were built on the northwest shore of Tybee Island. Construction of the batteries, gun platforms, magazines, and splinter-proof shelters; hauling supplies; and mounting the guns and mortars was all done at night, frequently in driving rain. All work was covered with brush before dawn to con-

under construction. Lieutenant Horace Porter supervised the landing of the guns and supplies and their transport across Tybee.

Work progressed slowly. Wooden platforms were constructed to hold the heavy guns. When the weight of the guns and their metal carriages cracked through the platforms, soldiers added iron tracks to reinforce the wood. Soldiers also constructed powder magazines and bombproofs and covered them with a thick layer of protective sand. A sheltered corduroy road connected the batteries.

Moving the guns and carriages was

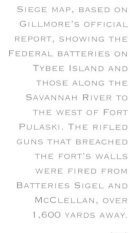

SIEGE MAP, BASED ON GILLMORE'S OFFICIAL REPORT, SHOWING THE FEDERAL BATTERIES ON TYBEE ISLAND AND THOSE ALONG THE SAVANNAH RIVER TO THE WEST OF FORT PULASKI. THE RIFLED GUNS THAT BREACHED THE FORT'S WALLS WERE FIRED FROM BATTERIES SIGEL AND MCCLELLAN, OVER 1,600 YARDS AWAY.

(BL)

ceal it from the Confederates. Once a safe parapet was complete, work could continue behind it with more freedom. Parties of men did mechanical tasks during the day; they arrived before daylight and returned to camp after dark. By the end of February most of the batteries were

difficult. The men worked at night. Teams of up to 250 men pulled the sling carts. Commands were conveyed by whistles: stop, start, slacken the ropes. The last mile was over boggy ground and wheels would sometimes slip into the mud and sink five feet to their hubs. If the cart could not be levered back onto the road, the gun tube was cut loose and rolled onto firmer ground and then reattached to the sling cart. All of this was done in the dark without a word spoken. Slowly, over seven weeks the soldiers completed the batteries and placed the guns. They unloaded powder, shot, and shells at the small island wharf. These were stored near the lighthouse and in magazines sited near the batteries.

Gillmore had requested ten rifled guns for experimental use during the bombardment. Familiar with published reports of European trials, he wished to use the rifled guns against masonry Fort Pulaski. He originally located the guns too far to the east and it was through the cajoling of one of his engineer assistants, Horace Porter, that he eventually came to move them to the batteries closest to the fort. Had Gillmore initially believed the rifled guns would have been effective in reducing the fort, he would not have spent seven weeks moving the heavy mortars and columbiads into place before beginning the bombardment of Pulaski.

Confederates were suspicious of the apparent inactivity on Tybee Island. On the night of March 22 three rebels slipped across the south channel of the Savannah River and discovered a Federal battery. At 10:00 P.M. the scouts delivered their report to Olmstead, who immediately ordered the fort to fire at the western end of the island. At dawn, he was unable to see if he had caused any damage. Although Pulaski's guns caused no problems for the Federals, Olmstead now knew that the Federals were preparing for a bombardment.

On March 30 a group from the 46th New York on a reconnaissance along

Wilmington Narrows were captured by members of the 13th Georgia. The Yankees "made little resistance & seem perfectly well satisfied to be captives." Several prisoners described the batteries, as well as their armament, for the anticipated bombardment of the fort. The *Savannah Republican* published the information the following day, and couriers slipped across the marsh and through the Federal lines and brought the information to Colonel Olmstead on April 4. By now,

of course, the isolated Confederates could do nothing but wait.

General Thomas Sherman was unpopular with many of his subordinate officers. He also was criticized in the Northern press for his seeming inactivity. By March 1862, he had secured Port Royal Sound, Hilton Head, and the surrounding South Carolina islands, Tybee Island, and in early March the port of Fernandina, Florida. His three brigades were stretched thinly. Although he could raid the interior, he did not have sufficient men to move inland and permanently occupy any more territory. Efforts of the troops on Tybee had been kept from the Northern newspapers by an embargo on letters going north. Finally, however, the War Department gave in to popular clamor and replaced Sherman with Major General David Hunter.

Hunter had graduated from the United States Military Academy in 1822. He had served fourteen years, resigned, and returned to serve as paymaster during the Mexican War. A politically active abolitionist, he had accompanied Lincoln's party to the District of Columbia for the 1861 inauguration. Slightly wounded in the Battle of First Manassas, he had then replaced Major General John C. Frémont in Missouri, where he brought relative order to the chaos of Frémont's regime.

Accompanying Hunter was Brigadier

General Henry W. Benham, an 1837 graduate of the United States Military Academy. An engineer officer, Benham had made his career with the army. Although highly regarded as an engineer,

he had not thus far distinguished himself in the war.

Hunter and Benham arrived at Port Royal Sound on March 31. Sherman briefed Hunter on the state of affairs, especially the progress of works against Fort Pulaski. Hunter immediately began reorganizing his Department of the South, which included Federally controlled enclaves in Georgia and Florida. He placed Benham in command of the Northern District, which covered the same territory previously commanded by Sherman. Sherman briefed Benham in detail about preparations against Pulaski. Hunter then officially thanked Sherman, and shortly thereafter Sherman departed for a new assignment in the West.

Although Sherman had not been a popular commander, Du Pont, who had worked with him longest, reflected:

poor fellow, a more onerous, difficult, responsible, but thankless piece of work no officer ever had to do, and none ever brought to such a task more complete self-sacrificing devotion—he ploughed, harrowed, sowed, and it does seem hard that when the crop was about being harvested he is not even allowed to participate in a secondary position.

Since Benham's new areas of responsibility covered exactly those of Sherman, Du Pont felt this gave "more point to the recall, or rather making it [a] recall which was unnecessary if not unjust."

Benham immediately met with Gillmore to review plans for the bombardment of Fort Pulaski. Gillmore remained Benham's chief engineer; Porter, his chief of ordnance. On April 1, Benham inspected the works on Tybee Island. He pressed Gillmore to complete the Tybee batteries; Benham was concerned about the lack of additional batteries at other sites that could provide concentric fire against the fort from opposite quarters. He ordered a mortar battery on the eastern end of Long Island and began reviewing the possibilities of battery sites on the South Carolina islands north of Fort Pulaski.

The Confederates continued preparing for the coming bombardment. By now the blindage against many of the casemate doors had been covered with heaped dirt. In early April the garrison pulled down the colonnade in front of the officers' quarters and mess rooms. They deepened the trenches on the parade.

Squat piles of sandbag traverses sat between the parapet guns. One Confederate recorded in his diary that he put his trust "in God, ourselves, the mosquitos & sand flies."

On the afternoon of April 9, a small party of Confederates slipped out of Fort Pulaski and rowed to Long Island, a mile and a half from the fort, where they discovered the mortar battery. Disabling the mortar by driving a tenpenny nail into the fuse hole, they returned to the fort with shells, powder, fuses, and other artillery supplies.

Beginning in April the Connecticut and New York men began intensive drills on the guns. Instructed by the Rhode

Island artillerymen, they practiced everything but firing. The infantrymen were under a distinct disadvantage because they were unable to get the range of their pieces before the bombardment opened. Many of the Federal officers were not optimistic about the success of the bombardment and feared that if it dragged on for long, a Confederate ironclad, then known to be under construction in Savannah, might pass Batteries Vulcan

THIS 1863 PHOTOGRAPH SHOWS FORT PULASKI AFTER ITS SURRENDER. THE 3D RHODE ISLAND HEAVY ARTILLERY ARE AT PRACTICE WITH SMOOTHBORE AND SIEGE GUNS.

(USAMHI)

14

FORTIFICATION IN THE CIVIL WAR

Fort Pulaski was part of a large system of fortifications that by 1860 guarded virtually every important harbor in the United States. As such, it reflected an outlook that for nearly two centuries dominated American military policy. With the army small and scattered over the frontier, coastal fortification in fact was about as much military policy as the country was willing to implement.

The first act of the first English colonists in Virginia in 1607 was to build a fort. As the colonies expanded in the following centuries, so did their penchant for fortifying any place deemed threatened or useful as a refuge. By the time

the Americans declared their independence from Britain in 1776, they were decidedly fortification-minded. This outlook was reinforced after independence by the Founding Fathers' distaste for professional armies, as well as anxiety about threats from Britain or other European nations. Forts offered physical strength at threatened points and would bolster the militia who would rush to meet an attack. The navy was the country's first line of defense, and forts protected naval refuges.

The first fortification program of the new nation was a series of simple earthworks erected to meet a threat of war with France in the 1790s. A decade later, increasing

tensions with Britain called for a more sophisticated set of installations, the first public work partly conducted by engineers American in birth and training—the early graduates of the United States Military Academy at West Point.

The war that erupted in 1812 between the United States and Britain saw few American successes, except for repulses of the enemy from fortified places such as Craney Island in Virginia and Fort McHenry in Maryland. The country was invaded several times, and only forts and fieldworks offered any bright spots in a dismal story. The legacy of the War of 1812 dominated military policy thereafter, in two respects—the country was vulnerable to invasion, and forts answered that danger.

Over the next half-century, army engineers erected works at every major and many minor harbors along the Atlantic and Gulf coasts and, after 1850, on the Pacific as well. Like Pulaski, they were sophisticated exercises in geometry and masonry, expressions of principles worked out in European siege warfare and perfected in the seventeenth and eighteenth centuries. They were no match, however,

and Hamilton and jeopardize the Federal endeavor.

Hunter initially planned to open on the fort on April 9, but torrential rain fell all day. He postponed the bombardment. The day was spent rushing preparations for an opening the next day. Bags of powder for the 13-inch mortars had not arrived; the men would have to measure powder with empty vegetable cans, pour it loose into the guns, and adjust it in the chamber before firing. Columbiad shells were bound to wooden sabots, or disks, with strips of tent canvas; the sabots were at the end of the

shell opposite the fuse hole and served to orient the ball, fuse away from the charge, before firing. That night the Federals suddenly discovered they had no fuse plugs for their 10-inch mortar shells. The Connecticut men sat up during the night whittling mortar fuses; after seven weeks' exertions hauling guns and building batteries, they were content to sit and whittle.

The Federals on Tybee Island had constructed eleven batteries containing 36 artillery pieces. Benham later remarked that Gillmore had named the batteries for "the persons most prominent *or most like-*

for advances in military and industrial technology happening in the nineteenth century.

The forts were built to withstand solid shot fired by smoothbore cannons. The advent of explosive rounds fired by rifled guns spelled their doom. As Union gunners demonstrated at Fort Pulaski in 1862, rifled shot could penetrate fort walls, exploding within amid a shower of splinters. The smoking holes in Pulaski's walls looked out on the end of an era.

There was some attempt to reinforce the forts to meet the new realities after the Civil War, but by 1875 they were mostly abandoned. Advances in metallurgy, explosives, gun design, and shipbuilding went on apace, and in the 1880s the country began another attempt

to fortify itself. Modern gun emplacements appeared at harbors around the country, but they nearly always were outmoded before completion. Still the country turned to fortifications with new types in the 1930s and 1940s.

Forts, however, were yesterday's answer to tomorrow's

challenges, which now came from above. They received their ultimate insult during the Japanese attack on Pearl Harbor, Hawaii, in 1941, after which it was apparent that fixed coastal emplacements—whether Fort Pulaski or something newer—no longer met the need. The last expression of fort-mindedness was the NIKE missile antiaircraft installations of the 1950s, mostly abandoned within a decade.

Fort Pulaski exemplifies an important and long-standing part of America's military past. Its dramatically sudden obsolescence in 1862 reflected more than the end of an era, however. It signaled the birth of modern warfare.

— *David A. Clary*

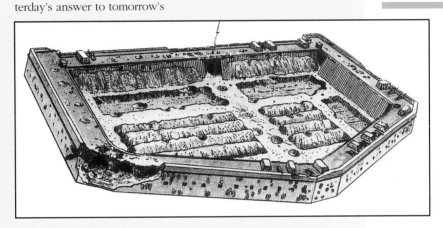

ly to be so, in political or military service." The batteries, their armament, and distance from Fort Pulaski are listed below:

Battery	Armament	Distance to Pulaski, yds.
Stanton	3 13-inch mortars	3,400
Grant	3 13-inch mortars	3,200
Lyon	3 10-inch mortars	3,100
Lincoln	3 8-inch mortars	3,045
Burnside	1 13-inch mortar	2,750
Sherman	3 13-inch mortars	2,650
Halleck	2 13-inch mortars	2,400
Scott	3 10-inch columbiads	1,740
	1 8-inch columbiad	
Sigel	5 30-pounder Parrotts	1,670
	1 48-pounder James rifle	
	(old 24-pounder)	
McClellan	2 84-pounder James rifles	1,650
	(old 42-pounder)	
	2 64-pounder James rifles	
	(old 32-pounder)	
Totten	4 10-inch mortars	1,650

Close to each battery was a service magazine filled with sufficient powder for two days' firing. Nine hundred shot and shells for each gun were also stored in the service magazines. A depot magazine

near the lighthouse held an additional 3,600 barrels of powder. Traverses separated the guns in each battery, protecting the gun crews from lateral explosions. Each battery had splinterproofs for the shifts of men not on duty. Each battery had its own well. The advanced batteries were all connected by trenches for safe communication. A bombproof surgery was erected at Goat Point, near Lazaretto Creek, also the site of the four batteries closest to Fort Pulaski.

That night Gillmore issued his final instructions, coordinating the role of each battery. The eastern mortar batteries and Battery Totten were to drop their shells on the parapet above the casemates to penetrate the earth and collapse the

underlying arches. Columbiads in Batteries Lyon and Lincoln were to fire over the southeast wall and hit the interior of the the gorge and north face. Batteries Scott and Lyon's columbiads were to help silence the barbette guns and then direct their fire at the *pan coupé* between the south and southeast faces. The rifled guns of Battery Sigel were to incapacitate the barbette guns, then direct their efforts to breach the *pan coupé*. The rifled guns in Battery McClellan were to fire directly at the *pan coupé* to attempt to breach the wall.

That night Hunter and Benham sailed from Port Royal Sound to Tybee; Hunter anchored near the lighthouse early on the morning of April 10. Hunter had invited Du Pont to accompany them, but the commodore regarded it as "an army affair" at which he had no business. While Benham made his final inspection, Hunter remained aboard his boat to prepare his summons for Olmstead's surrender. Horace Porter noted the arrival of the two new "stars," a reference to their shoulder straps of rank, and noted that they were "as impatient for the fray as Roman ladies for the commencements of a gladiatorial combat."

As light dawned at 5:30 on the morning of April 10 Confederates in Fort Pulaski discovered that mounds of sand at

the west end of Tybee Island had been leveled, brush cut away, and four batteries stood where dunes had been visible before. Only part of Pulaski's artillery—ten barbette guns, six casemate guns, and two mortars—could fire on Tybee. Only four barbette guns and three casemate guns could bear on Goat Point, site of the Federal rifled guns, four columbiads, and four mortars.

At dawn Hunter sent Lieutenant Wilson over to the fort to demand its surrender. Four sailors rowed Wilson over to Cockspur Island; Wilson sat in the bow and an additional sailor in the stern held aloft a white flag. Hunter's terms of surrender read:

I hereby demand of you the immediate surrender and restoration of Fort Pulaski to the authority and possession of the United States. This demand is made with a view of avoiding, if possible, the effusion of blood which must result from the bombardment and attack now in readiness to be opened.

The number, caliber, and completeness of the batteries surrounding you leave no doubt as to what must result in case of your refusal; and as the defense, however obstinate, must eventually succumb to the assailing force at my disposal, it is hoped you may see fit to avert the useless waste of life.

Wilson's orders allowed him to wait only thirty minutes for a reply. A Confederate lieutenant, also with a flag of truce, politely received Wilson at the

south wharf. Leaving Wilson with his boat, the Confederate returned to the fort. He rejoined Wilson exactly thirty minutes later with Colonel Olmstead's sealed reply. With the Federal batteries unmasked, Olmstead knew the moment he had awaited for two months was now arrived. He used his thirty minutes to assemble his men, post them to their guns, serve ammunition, and prepare the hospital. The colonel's message to Hunter was brief:

I have to acknowledge receipt of your communication of this date demanding the unconditional surrender of Fort Pulaski. In reply I can only say that I am here to defend the fort, not to surrender it.

I have the honor to be, very respectively, your obedient servant,
Chas. H. Olmstead
Colonel, First Volunteer Regiment of Georgia, commanding Post

Hunter read Olmstead's reply, then quickly sent an aide to Porter with the message, "The General sends his compliments and desires you open the ball at once." At 8:15 A.M., Porter aimed and fired the first gun, a 13-inch mortar in

Shortly before noon, the halyard of Pulaski's flagpole was cut by a shell and the flag fluttered down. Thinking the fort had surrendered, Federal soldiers mounted their parapets and cheered their victory.

A *HARPER'S WEEKLY* ILLUSTRATION OF THE ATTACK ON FORT PULASKI.

Battery Halleck. A member of the 7th Connecticut gun crew chalked on the side of the shell, "A nutmeg from Connecticut; can you furnish a grater?" The shell moved in a graceful arc over Pulaski and exploded on its descent beyond the fort. Confederate Lieutenant Henry Freeman offered the first response with a 32-pounder casemate gun. Initial firing on each side was slow and wild but each soon learned the range of his targets. Within an hour, the Federal batteries were firing three rounds a minute. The northwest shore of Tybee Island was a line of smoke punctuated with blasts of flame. The reverberation of fifty cannons from both sides made the ground shake. As the morning passed, the guns, especially those of the Federals, gained greater accuracy.

Colonel Rosa and members of his 46th New York manned the guns of Battery Sigel. Rosa disregarded his firing instructions, mounted the parapet, drew his sword, and directed all six guns to fire in one volley. Continuing to fire in volley with great cheers, the men made up in enthusiasm what they lacked in accuracy. Rosa was unable to control his men, ignored his orders, and "was making bad work of it" when Gillmore ordered him away. The New Yorkers refused to work their guns without their colonel, so Gillmore sent them all packing and

replaced them with sailors, trained on artillery, from Du Pont's *Wabash*.

Shortly before noon, the halyard of Pulaski's flagpole was cut by a shell and the flag fluttered down. Thinking the fort had surrendered, Federal soldiers mounted their parapets and cheered their victory. Confederates soon removed the tangled flag from the parapet and remounted it on a temporary staff—a cannon rammer—in the northeast angle of the fort. A volley at the Federals sent them scampering into their batteries and fire immediately resumed.

Confederate shells directed against the middle batteries frequently fell short, splashing into the river. The marshes behind the breaching batteries at Goat Point caught many Confederate mortar rounds, which sank before exploding.

Inside the fort, a shot came through a casemate embrasure early in the day, dismounting a gun and severely wounding one man. The James projectiles were flaking brick. Olmstead wrote, "Thirteen inch mortar shells, columbiad shells, Parrott shells, and rifle shots were shrieking through the air in every direction, while the ear was deafened by the tremendous explosions that followed each other without cessation." After three hours of firing three casemate guns lay dismounted. Most of the Confederate parapet guns, on the sea face, were dismounted by the end of the first day. "The effect upon the fortification was becoming disastrous," the colonel observed. Later during the first day of the bombardment, Olmstead was

in a casemate when a columbiad shot from Goat Point struck the fort while the wall was still intact and "bulged the bricks on the inside, a significant fact that left little doubt of what the ultimate result would be." By the end of the first day's bombardment, the wall had been flaked away and only two to four feet of brick remained.

During the night of the first day's bombardment, Olmstead went out to inspect the exterior of the fort:

It was worse then disheartening, the pan-coupe at the south-east angle was entirely breached while above, on the rampart, the parapet had been shot away and an 8-inch gun, the muzzle of which was gone, hung trembling over the verge. The two adjacent casemates were rapidly approaching the same ruined condition; masses of broken masonry nearly filled the moat. . . . [In] the interior of the three casemates . . . dismounted guns lay like logs among the bricks.

To his wife, Olmstead wrote that the angle opposite the Goat Point batteries was shattered and that he knew that "another day would breach it entirely."

Federal fire continued during the night, one round every ten or fifteen minutes to prevent the defenders from sleeping. Early the next morning, both sides resumed in earnest. Only three Confederate parapet guns bore on Tybee and only one could reach the Goat Point batteries. Benham and his staff, standing on a dune behind Battery Lyon, observed progress through a large tripod telescope.

They saw the growing pile of rubble overflowing the moat. Shells from rifled guns penetrated deeper and deeper, fracturing the brick wall. Solid shot from the columbiads smashed the masonry, dislodging great slides of brick into the moat amid rust-colored clouds. One Federal observed that with each shot that struck the wall "a cart-load of brick [would] fall into the ditch." By 10:00 A.M. Benham could see the thinnest wall of a recess arch at the angle. An hour or so later the next arch was visible. Toward noon three casemate arches were opened. Gillmore now ordered the guns to begin concentrating on the next adjacent casemate wall along the southeast wall.

By now great masses of brick, loosened the previous day, filled the moat. With the first visible opening, Tybee Island rang with "cheer after cheer." "What a scream ran down the line when the first hole appeared! Every shot that

enlarged it was hailed with another yell." Another Federal officer reported that "soon a huge opening appeared in the wall through which a two horse wagon might have been driven." Excited gunners redoubled their rate of fire and it seemed as if "even the solid earth shook with the long thunder peal."

It was now apparent that the face of the southeast wall would be peeled off. With the moat filled with brick debris, an assault party, aided by ladders, could scramble over the rubble and into the fort and overpower the garrison, the strength of which Federals had learned earlier from deserters. Benham's aide, Major Charles G. Halpine, was assigned to lead the assault. Knowing that two Irish companies were in the fort, the Irishman Halpine wanted to lead the column. Scheduled for April 12, the assault would prove unnecessary.

During the morning of the second day a Confederate shell burst over a gun in Battery McClellan mortally wounding Private Thomas Campbell, Company H, of the 3d Rhode Island Heavy Artillery. Horace Porter observed that "his face was burned perfectly black, his left side torn away and his left leg taken off. He lived three hours, spoke about his wife and family, seized hold of his captain's hand and died." Campbell was the only Federal fatality of the bombardment.

Inside Pulaski, Olmstead realized that "it was simply a question of a few hours as to whether we should yield or be blown into perdition by our own powder." By now seven barbette guns were disabled, the traverses were "giving way," the west side of the fort was a wreck, and the southeast angle was badly breached, allowing "free access of every shot to our magazine." The magazine, in the northwest corner, was protected by a large traverse;

however, around 1:00 P.M. a shell entered an opened casemate at the southeast angle, passed across the parade, and through the top of the traverse to explode in the entrance way of the magazine. The magazine was piled high with barrels of powder—twenty tons. The magazine filled with light and smoke but did not explode. Olmstead knew that the next such shot could blow up the fort beneath them all. He realized he had reached the end. Beyond any help from the "Confederate Authorities," he "did not feel warranted in exposing the garrison to the hazard of the blowing up of our main magazine. . . . There are times when a soldier must hold his position 'to the last extremity,' which means *extermination*, but this was not one of them, there was no end to be gained by continued resistance."

Confederate fire ceased at 2:00 P.M., the Confederate flag was lowered, and a white flag was raised. All but two parapet guns were disabled; two casemate guns bearing on Tybee Island were dismounted. The outer wall covering two casemates had been destroyed and that of the adjoining casemate on either side was crumbling. Incredibly, only three Confederates— A. Shaw, T. J. Moullon, and Isaac Ames— were seriously wounded.

Benham and members of his staff gathered at Lazaretto Creek to find a boat to take them over to Pulaski. A violent storm had blown throughout the eleventh and the soldiers were unable to get their boat away. Gillmore had joined Benham's party to cross to Cockspur Island and accept the surrender; he left and found some of the *Wabash* sailors, who, understanding tides and currents, quickly rowed him to the fort. He entered, had the gates shut, and met with Olmstead for an hour

arranging the terms of surrender. When the other Federal officers, led by Halpine, were finally able to reach Cockspur Island, Gillmore kept them waiting outside the fort until he had the signed surrender document:

ARTICLE 1. The fort, armament, and garrison to be surrendered at once to the forces of the United States.

ART. 2. The officers and men of the garrison to be allowed to take with them all their private effects, such as clothing, bedding, books, &c.; this not to include private weapons.

ART. 3. The sick and wounded, under charge of the hospital steward of the garri-

HEAVY TIMBERS OR BLINDAGE COVERED THE CONFEDERATE LIVING QUARTERS, PROTECTING THEM FROM EXPLODING SHELLS.

(NPS)

INTERIOR OF ONE OF THE RUINED CASEMENTS AFTER THE SURRENDER OF FORT PULASKI.

(LC)

son, to be sent up under a flag of truce to the Confederate lines, and at the same time the men to be allowed to send up any letters they may desire, subject to the inspection of a Federal officer.

Gillmore left the fort as Halpine and his party entered to take charge of the surrender of the fort and receive the officers' swords and take possession of the flag.

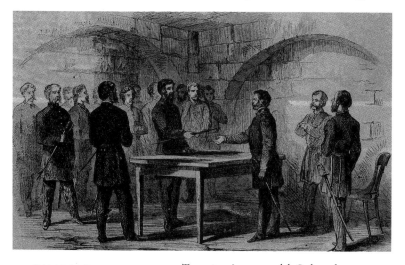

Twenty-six-year-old Colonel Olmstead handled the surrender gracefully. He impressed all as "a man of superior character. . . . reflective countenance, and mild and gentlemanly manners." Once the garrison had been assembled to stack arms, Olmstead asked if he might be spared ordering his men to disarm. Halpine gave the necessary orders. Next the officers surrendered their swords and sidearms. Olmstead stepped forward first, placed his sword on the table, and said, "I yield my sword, but I trust I have not disgraced it." The other officers came forward according to rank and laid their swords on the table, "most of them making a slight inclination of the head and showing good bearing." A few sullenly threw their swords down. One said, "I hope to be able to resume it to fight for the same cause." Another officer claimed to have no sword and offered to surrender his sash, which was refused.

After the ceremony was finished, the officers adjourned to the mess room where food and wine were served. Feelings of awkwardness lifted during the informal conversation. One Confederate officer joked, "Why you are only four and we three hundred and fifty; I think we ought to take you." Another Confederate sarcastically asked a Connecticut officer about wooden nutmegs. Pointing to a 10-inch columbiad shot, the Northerner answered, "We don't make them out of wood any longer." Altogether, 361 Confederates surrendered, 24 of whom were officers. Eighteen sick or wounded Confederates would remain in the fort; the remainder were sent north to prison. Contrary to the surrender terms, the prisoners were not allowed to take their

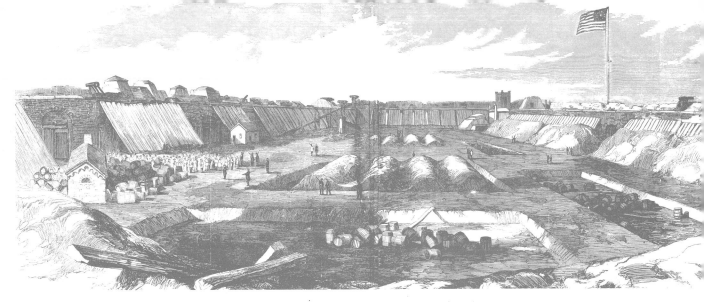

private effects with them into captivity. Those remaining in the hospital were not returned to Confederate authorities but, when well enough, were sent north to prison. The officers and men were exchanged in August and September 1862 and again served the Confederacy. Years after the war, Colonel Olmstead was offered the opportunity to meet with Gillmore; the Georgian declined because he felt that Gillmore had allowed Hunter to violate the terms of surrender.

The 7th Connecticut immediately occupied the fort. Lieutenant Colonel Joseph Hawley, of the 7th Connecticut, retrieved the white surrender flag and sent it to his wife. Officers cut the Confederate flag into fragments and sent them home as souvenirs of their victory. It had been a year since the bombardment of Fort Sumter; Horace Porter wrote his sister, "Sumter is avenged!" Along with members of the 1st New York Volunteer Engineers, the Connecticut men began repairing the breach and by the end of April the repair work was well under way; it was completed the following month. Guns were removed from Tybee Island and shipped northward, some destined for the siege of Fort Sumter. Batteries Vulcan and Hamilton on the Savannah River were disarmed. On June 4, the 48th New York replaced the 7th

Connecticut; they remained for almost a year. In June 1863, Pulaski's garrrison was reduced.

Federals had fired over five thousand projectiles; the Confederates, a third that many. Gillmore observed that the 84-pound solid James projectiles had penetrated up to twenty-six inches. The lighter James projectiles had penetrated twenty inches. Most of the damage was caused by three James rifles—two 84-pounders and one 64-pounder. The Parrott projectiles penetrated up to eighteen inches; however, they frequently wobbled and flipped end over end and were of little use in the bombardment.

The columbiads had less penetrating power but were most effective, "crushing out immense masses of masonry." Fewer than 10 percent of the mortar rounds even hit the fort. The mortars caused

INTERIOR OF THE FORT AS IT LOOKED ON APRIL 12, THE DAY AFTER ITS BOMBARDMENT.

(FL)

THE BAND OF THE 48TH NEW YORK VOLUNTEER INFANTRY INSIDE THE OCCUPIED FORT.

(USAMHI)

none of the anticipated damage to the casemate arches. As effective as the Federal artillery was, it would have been even more so had the crews been given opportunity to drill and fire their artillery pieces before the actual bombardment.

The effectiveness of rifled artillery meant that future sieges and bombardments could be prepared for far more easily. Instead of seven weeks of heavy labor preparing batteries and moving heavy mortars and columbiads, lighter rifled guns could be more quickly maneuvered into position. Rifled guns would play a major role in Gillmore's next endeavor—the siege and bombardment of Fort Sumter in Charleston Harbor.

The use of rifled artillery revolutionized siege warfare. Before the reduction of Fort Pulaski, masonry forts were regarded as impregnable. Major General David Hunter best summarized the significance of what happened on Cockspur Island:

The result of this bombardment must cause, I am convinced, a change in the construction of fortifications as radical as that foreshadowed in naval architecture by the conflict between the Monitor *and* Merrimac. *No works of stone or brick can resist the impact of rifled artillery of heavy caliber.*

After its capture, Fort Pulaski played little active role in the war. It closed Savannah as a Confederate port. Held by a reduced garrison,

UNION SOLDIERS PROUDLY POSE IN ONE OF THE GAPING HOLES CAUSED BY THE CONSTANT BOMBARDMENT.

(LC)

it would gain brief noteriety during 1864. In June, the Confederate commander in Charleston, South Carolina, Major General Samuel Jones, attempting to relieve the bombardment of his city, placed five generals and forty-five field officers in quarters in parts of the city that had been under constant shelling. He then notified Major General John G. Foster, commander of the Department of the South. Foster retaliated immediately, requested a similar number of Confederate prisoners of equal rank, and placed them in a stockade on Morris Island under the guns of Fort Sumter. Jones soon realized that his strategy had served no useful end; however, it suddenly became difficult to move the prisoners from Charleston. Major General William T. Sherman had begun his campaign into northwest Georgia and the Confederate prisoner of war camp in Andersonville was believed to be among his possible objectives. Hundreds of

THE SOUTHEASTERN WALL WITH THE BREACHED *PAN COUPÉ* ON THE LEFT. RUBBLE NEARLY FILLS THE MOAT AT THE POINT OF THE BREACH.

(USAMHI)

Federal prisoners were transferred elsewhere, and many began to arrive daily in Charleston. Jones's problem suddenly changed when a yellow fever epidemic erupted in the city. He was able now to transfer his prisoners—officers to Columbia and men to Florence, South Carolina—without authorization from his superiors.

Foster had accumulated 600 Rebel prisoners before the crisis passed. Forty-nine were hospitalized, four had escaped, two had taken the Oath of Allegiance to the United States, two had been exchanged, four were dead, six were imprisoned elsewhere for attempting to escape, and thirteen were "unaccounted for." Foster sent his 520 bedraggled men to Fort Pulaski for imprisonment. Shoeless, dressed in rags, they were ill with dysentery and pneumonia.

Colonel Philip P. Brown, of the 157th New York, now commanded the fort. Knowing the prisoners were coming, he requisitioned blankets, clothing, and firewood. His requests were ignored. Confined in the casemates within an iron prison cage, the Confederates had neither blankets nor decent clothes. Coal was absent and firewood scarce; cookstoves could be lit only once a day. Colonel Brown fed the prisoners as well as he could from the garrison stores, for which he was censured by his commanding general.

After conditions in Andersonville prison became known, Federal authorities retaliated. On December 15 Brown was ordered to impose a starvation ration: a quarter pound of bread, ten ounces of cornmeal, and a half pint of pickles daily and one ounce of salt every five days.

Brown was instructed to allow the prisoners to purchase additional food from sutlers, but they had no money to do so. Further, Brown was not allowed to receive money from Confederate authorities.

Winter was unusually severe. The prisoners subsisted on their bread, cornmeal, and pickles. Rats and an occasional stray dog or cat added to their diet. There were no blankets and no fires. The men began to succumb to scurvy in mid-January.

THE SOUTHWEST CORNER OF FORT PULASKI, 1863.

(USAMHI)

Savannah fell to Union authorities on December 21, 1864, and by January 21, 1865, Fort Pulaski was assigned to Major General Cuvier Grover's District of Savannah. Six days later, the district's medical director inspected the fort and the prisoners were immediately returned to full rations. Four hundred and sixty-five—all that survived—were sent north on March 5, 1865, to the Federal prison at Fort Delaware.

In May 1865, the captured president of the Confederate States, Jefferson Davis, was briefly imprisoned in Fort Pulaski. In command of the detail escorting Davis northward was Brigadier General James

H. Wilson, who had served during the preparations to isolate, besiege, and bombard Fort Pulaski earlier in the war. During the summer three Confederate cabinet officers—Secretary of State Robert M. T. Hunter, Secretary of the Treasury George A. Trenholm, and Secretary of War James H. Seddon—were imprisoned in the fort. Confederate assistant secretary

mouth of Cape Fear River, are examples of large earthen forts that withstood prolonged, heavy bombardment.

The earthen fort at Genesis Point on the Great Ogeechee River was begun in 1861 as the southernmost part of the Savannah inner defense line. It was designed to protect the Savannah, Albany and Gulf Railroad as well as the rice plan-

PAINTING OF TODAY'S
FORT PULASKI FROM
THE WEST SHOWS THE
PLAN OF THE FORT.
STRUCTURES IN THE
DEMILUNE WERE BUILT
DECADES AFTER THE
CIVIL WAR.

(NPS)

of war John A. Campbell, Alabama governor Andrew B. Moore, South Carolina governor Andrew G. Magrath, Florida governor Alexander K. Allison, and Florida senator David L. Yulee were all confined during 1865.

THE ATTACK ON FORT McALLISTER

Rifled artillery rendered masonry fortifications like Fort Pulaski obsolete. Sprawling, untidy earth fortifications, thrown up by both sides during the Civil War, now proved themselves to be the impregnable defenses. Fort Wagner, on Morris Island, and Fort Fisher, at the

tations along the river. Although General Robert E. Lee visited the site during his command of the Confederate Department of South Carolina, Georgia, and Florida, the ultimate design must be credited to Captain John McCrady, who applied the lessons learned from the rapid breaching of Fort Pulaski. Each gun in McAllister was separated by a large traverse, beneath which was located a magazine. In the center of the fort was a huge bombproof. Sandwiched between the traverses, each gun was shielded in a protective valley. A Union naval officer stated in 1864 that it was "so crammed with bomb proofs and traverses as to look as if the spaces were carved out of solid earth."

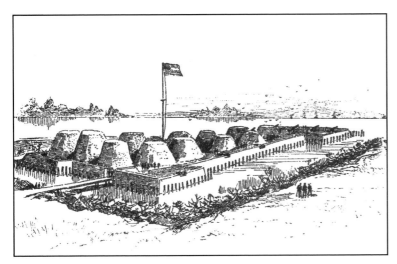

From the time of its construction the fort saw no activity until July 1862. That month the Confederate sidewheel blockade runner *Nashville*, unable to dash into Charleston, eluded her pursuers after a long chase and slipped into the Ogeechee River. Guided through the pilings that diagonally crossed the river a third of a mile below the fort, she came to rest above Fort McAllister. Federal naval officers would keep her from leaving for eight months until they could destroy her. To reach the *Nashville* they would have to silence Fort McAllister.

On July 1, 1862, the USS *Alabama*, a nine-gun sidewheel steamer, fired on Fort McAllister but withdrew before she was hit. At the end of the month, July 29, three gunboats, the six-gun *Unadilla*, the four-gun *Huron*, and the three-gun *Madgie*, fired on the fort for an hour and a half but neither caused nor received any damage. During the engagement, the sailors did not see the *Nashville*.

On November 19, 1862, the gunboats *Wissahickon* and *Dawn*, along with a mortar schooner, engaged Fort McAlister for almost five hours. The *Wissahickon* was hit below the waterline and "reluctantly dropped down beyond their range and succeeded in partially stopping the leak." Although Federal guns produced shell craters "large enough to bury a horse," they caused no permanent damage. The vessels left the *Nashville* bottled up.

Renewed efforts to reduce Fort McAllister began early the next year. On January 27, 1863, the *Montauk*, a two-gun monitor, along with the gunboats *Seneca*, *Wissahickon* and *Dawn* and the mortar schooner *C. P. Williams*, slowly steamed up the river and anchored 150 yards below the obstructing barrier of pilings. The *Montauk's* revolving turret was armed with eleven-inch and fifteen-inch Dahlgren guns, the latter the largest gun ever mounted on a warship. Similar in

Although Federal guns produced shell craters "large enough to bury a horse," they caused no permanent damage. The vessels left the Nashville bottled up.

The Montauk
opened at
7:45 A.M.
from 600
yards away.
For almost
five hours the
bombardment
continued.

COMMODORE
SAMUEL F. DU PONT

(USAMHI)

construction to the *Monitor*, she was commanded by the *Monitor*'s commander, John L. Worden.

Within 1,500 yards of the fort, the *Montauk* hurled its 400-pound projectiles at the fort for almost five hours before ending the engagement. All the while, the masts of the *Nashville* protruded above the trees on the neck of land that projected into the river curve. Although the *Montauk*'s shells tore into and through the twenty-foot-thick parapets, they caused no real damage and no casualties. Confederate guns hit the *Montauk* fifteen times but only dented her armor plate. Commodore Du Pont observed that "whatever degree of impenetrability they [ironclads] might have, there was no corresponding quality of aggression or destructiveness as against forts, the slowless of firing giving full time for the garrison in the fort to take shelter in the bomproof."

Monitor-class ships were new to the United States Navy, and before their deployment in Charleston Harbor, Commodore Du Pont wanted to evaluate their effectiveness against fortifications. Although relieved at the slight damage to the ironclad, Du Pont wondered "if one ironclad cannot take eight guns— how are five to take 147 guns in Charleston harbor." During the five days that elapsed, the Federals resupplied their vessels. The Confederates laid mines in the river near the pilings. On the twenty-ninth the Confederates burned the rice

and brush fields behind the fort to remove possible cover for a land attack. The *Nashville* dropped down to the vicinity of McAllister. Federal sailors could see the raider from the masts of their vessels.

On February 1, Worden made a second attempt to destroy the earth fort. The night before, using information obtained from runaway slaves, Federal crews removed the mines from the river. The Federal fleet, the *Montauk* and the four other vessels, were able to move closer than on the previous engagement. They could see no damage from the previous bombardment. The *Montauk* opened at 7:45 A.M. from 600 yards away. For almost five hours the bombardment continued. The *Montauk*, along with her escort gunboats, caused little damage. They were successful, inadvertently, in killing Major John B. Gallie, garrison commander. Confederates, in turn, hit the ironclad 48 times but caused more damage than in the first encounter. Colonel Robert H. Anderson, commander of Confederate forces along the Ogeechee, reported that "the enemy fired steadily and with remarkable precision. Their fire was terrible. Their mortar fire was unusually fine, a large number of their shells bursting directly over the battery. The ironclad's fire was principally directed at the VIII-inch Columbiad, and . . . the parapet in front of this gun was so badly breached as to leave it entirely exposed. . . . I think that the brave and heroic garrison of Fort McAllister have, after a most severe and trying fight, demonstrated to the world that victory does not, as a matter of course, always perch itself on the flag of an ironclad when opposed even to an ordinary earthwork manned by stout and gallant hearts."

Meanwhile, Confederate authorities had given up freeing the *Nashville* for further blockade-running duties and converted her into an armed commerce raider with the ominous name *Rattlesnake*. The Federals feared the *Rattlesnake* would be as dangerous as the *Alabama* had proved herself. At dusk on February 27, a cloudy and rainy day, she descended the river to try for the open sea but was deterred by the four-gun blockader *Seneca* and returned up the Ogeechee, only to go aground on a mud bank in a part of the river known as Seven-Mile Reach. Through their telescopes, Federals could see the *Rattlesnake's* crew moving busily on the decks and in the rigging trying to lighten her to float free. At 4:00 A.M. Worden prepared his men and signaled the *Seneca*, *Wissahickon*, and *Dawn* for a daylight attack. At 7:05 A.M. he anchored twelve hundred yards below the fort and about the same distance from the Confederate vessel, which was across the river bend. A Confederate tug was having no luck dislodging the *Rattlesnake*. The *Montauk* and *Rattlesnake* exchanged unequal fire over the half mile of marsh. An observer on the *Montauk* wrote:

At twenty-two minutes after seven we landed a fifteen-inch shell close to the Nashville, and five and one-half minutes later we sent another—it was our fifth shot—smashing into her hull, just between the foremast and paddlebox. Almost immediately followed the explosion. . . . Smoke settled about us, and after the eighth shot we ceased firing to let the air clear. Presently a breath of wind swept the drift aside, and we saw to our great joy a dense column of smoke rising from the forward deck of the stranded vessel. Our exploding shell had set her on fire. A few minutes more, and flames were distinctly visible, forcing their way up, gradually

creeping aft until they had reached nearly to the base of the smokestack.

Worden recorded that "at 9:20 a.m. a large pivot gun mounted abaft her foremast exploded from the heat; at 9:40 her smoke chimney went by the board, and at 9:55 her magazine exploded with terrific violence, shattering her in smoking ruins. Nothing remains of her."

Fort McAllister fired at the *Montauk* and the gunboats *Wissahickon* and *Dawn*, accompanying the ironclad, fired on the fort. The Federals damaged a barrack and plowed up the parade of the fort but little else.

As the vessels dropped down the river there was "a seemingly double explosion" as the *Montauk* shuddered, raised slightly in the water, and twisted violently. Although Worden initially thought a round from the fort had caused the damage, he quickly found that he had struck a mine. The ship quickly steered for a mudbank and beached, sealing the leak. The mine had caused a six-foot scar of separated, cracked plates and bent ribs. After temporary patching, the ironclad sailed to Port Royal for repairs.

On March 3, the Federal navy made one last attempt to reduce Fort McAllister. Three two-gun ironclads, the *Passaic*,

Nahant, and *Patapsco*, along with gunboats *Seneca*, *Wissahickon*, and *Dawn*, and mortar schooners *C. P. Williams*, *Para*, and *Norfolk Packet* moved up the Ogeechee. The mission was primarily gunnery training for the monitors in the coming campaign against Fort Sumter. Captain Percival Drayton, a South Carolinian who had remained loyal to the Union while his brother served as a Confederate general, commanded the squadron. The fort and gunboats exchanged fire for seven hours. The disappointed Drayton observed that there was no damage done that could not be repaired with "a good night's work." He added, "I do not believe that it can be made untenable by any number of ironclads . . . brought into position against it." The only casualty was the fort's mascot, "Tom Cat." The following day, no visible evidence of the bombardment remained. Unlike Fort Pulaski's masonry, the sand of Fort McAllister absorbed the impact of the bombardment. The damage could be shoveled back into place during the night.

The Union monitors made no further attacks on McAllister. The navy moved north to attempt to take Fort Sumter in Charleston Harbor. The garrison at McAllister shoveled dirt back onto the walls and waited for the next Federal move.

Unlike Fort Pulaski's masonry, the sand of Fort McAllister absorbed the impact of the bombardment. The damage could be shoveled back into place during the night.

UNION IRONCLADS *PATAPSCO, PASSAIC,* AND *NAHANT* SHELL FORT MCALLISTER ON MARCH 3, 1863.

(FL)

SHERMAN'S MARCH TO THE SEA

The next threat to Fort McAllister was from the land side. Major General William T. Sherman approached the city of Savannah at the conclusion of his famous march to the sea. Sherman had taken Atlanta, Georgia, as part of the Federal 1864 spring offensive. He began his southeast advance in mid-November. His 62,000-man army was divided into two "wings." The right wing was commanded by Major General Oliver O. Howard and was composed of two corps, the XV Corps commanded by Major General Peter J. Osterhaus and the XVII Corps led by Major General Frank P. Blair.

The left wing was commanded by Major General Henry W. Slocum and consisted of Brigadier General Jefferson C. Davis's XIV Corps and Brigadier General Alpheus S. Williams's XX Corps. Brigadier General Judson Kilpatrick commanded the cavalry. A pontoon train and a few companies of engineers, along with fifteen batteries of light artillery, accompanied the army.

Kilpatrick's cavalry and Howard's two corps moved south toward Macon; Slocum's wing headed east toward Augusta. Confederate Major General Gustavus W. Smith's force of a few thousand Georgia militia and local defense troops, along with a few brigades of Major General Joseph Wheeler's cavalry— 8,000 men—were south of Atlanta at Lovejoy Station and withdrew to Macon as the Federals marched out of Atlanta. On November 20 Howard abandoned his feint on Macon and moved toward Georgia's capital at Milledgeville. Confederate Lieutenant General William J. Hardee, headquartered in Savannah, commanded west to central Georgia and ordered Smith to move his force east to stand between Sherman's army and Augusta. As part of the move, Confederate Brigadier General Pleasant J. Phillips's three brigades of militia inadvertently collided with Union Brigadier General Charles C. Walcutt's rear-guard brigade of the XV Corps near Griswoldville. Phillips attacked the well-entrenched Union troops and was repulsed with over 500 casualties; Walcutt sustained less than 100 killed and wounded and continued on to Milledgeville.

On November 24 Sherman moved on to the Ogeechee River; five days later the Federals entered Louisville. Wheeler's troops, in an occasional skirmish, were their only opposition. By December 3, Sherman had reached Millen, almost 70 miles from the coast at Savannah or Unionist-controlled Port Royal Sound. Alarmed Confederates in Savannah began in earnest to fortify the western approaches to the city. Reinforcements from Georgia as well as the Carolinas were

SHERMAN'S TROOPS BEGIN THEIR "MARCH TO THE SEA" AS ATLANTA BURNS BEHIND THEM.

(FMTW)

Port Royal Sound to Boyd's Neck, ten miles east of the railroad at Grahamville. Hatch and his 5,500 men spent November 29 fortifying their position. His way was "blocked" by a few companies of the 3d South Carolina Cavalry. The following morning Hatch's command moved toward Grahamville. By now a large force on Confederates, including elements of Gustavus Smith's Georgia militia from Savannah, as well as troops from Charleston, had been concentrated in the South Carolina village. Smith moved some of his men to Honey Hill, three miles south of Grahamville. There, 1,400 men, along with five artillery pieces, dug in. Hatch's force was delayed by the Confederates, who set the fields and woods afire to confine the Federals to the road. Hindered by "dense undergrowth and swamps," the Unionists made little progress. By afternoon the Federals began to withdraw and by 7:30 they had retreated from the field. Hatch suffered over 750 casualties; Smith, less than 50.

moved into Savannah. Smith's militia reached the city early on November 30.

Union forces, anticipating Sherman's arrival on the coast, moved from Hilton Head inland to cut the Savannah and Charleston Railroad east of Grahamville, South Carolina. Major General John G. Foster, commander of the Department of the South headquartered at Hilton Head Island, ordered Brigadier General John P. Hatch to move up the Broad River from

This map shows the route of Sherman's destructive march to the sea. From Savannah, Sherman would head north to Charleston, South Carolina.

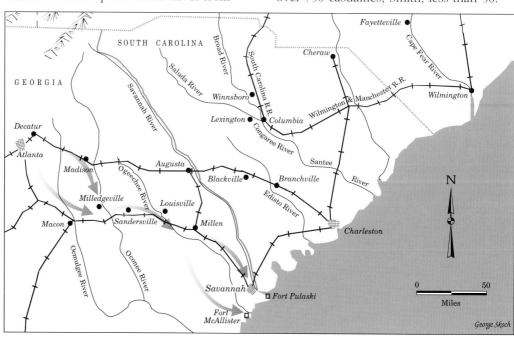

UNION TROOPS BURN A
RAILROAD BRIDGE OVER
THE OGEECHEE RIVER
ON NOVEMBER 30.

(FL)

As reinforcements continued to arrive in South Carolina, Smith and his militia returned to the Savannah defenses. Major General Samuel Jones, headquartered in Charleston, moved down the railroad as far as Pocotaligo. Jones's line would become the second front for Savannah. Although the Federals gained several positions from which they could shell the railroad, they never severed the Charleston and Savannah Railroad. The Federal failure to sever the railroad would result in a loss of the opportunity to trap Hardee and his forces in Savannah.

Meanwhile, as Sherman approached Savannah, Hardee prepared his defenses. He commanded about 10,000 troops and had no chance to defeat Sherman. His only hope was that Sherman, without supply lines, would be unable to subject the city to a prolonged siege and be forced to seek the Federal navy and supplies elsewhere, perhaps at Beaufort, South Carolina, the closest point under Federal control. Hardee,

however, hoped to retain control of the Charleston and Savannah Railroad, which extended about twenty miles from the city before turning north to cross the Savannah River. His outer line of defenses extended from the Savannah River above the bridge southwest to the Great Ogeechee River. Swamps and a few detached works, containing artillery, constituted the line.

Sherman left Millen on December 4 with three of his corps moving between the Ogeechee and Savannah Rivers. Osterhaus's XV Corps moved down the right bank of the Ogeechee River and thereby flanked Hardee's outer line, forcing him back to the inner line of defenses.

The right of the Confederate inner line extended on the right from

CONFEDERATE
BATTERIES LIKE THIS
ONE SURROUNDED
SAVANNAH.

(AMERICAN HERITAGE
COLLECTION)

Hardee stated that he had no plans to evacuate Savannah but that if it became necessary, he planned to use the Savannah River gunboats to ferry his men to South Carolina.

Williamson's Plantation on the Savannah River north of the city, near the upper end of Hutchinson Island, across high ground to the Little Ogeechee River. Much of the front was swamp and flooded rice fields. Two railroads and three wagon roads penetrated the defenses; they had been cut and stood under several feet of water. Fort Hardeman on the Savannah River protected the canal that allowed flooding of the rice fields. Battery McBeth covered the railroad as it passed through the central Confederate works. Piney Point Battery and Battery Jones covered the roads from the southwest. Confederates occupied the lower end of Hutchinson Island, covering the right flank of the inner line. Artillery from some of the river batteries east of the city was moved to protect against the threat of Federal land forces; 54 guns were moved after November 20.

The right of the Confederate was occupied by G. W. Smith's 2,000-man militia and 20 pieces of artillery; they extended to the Georgia Central Railroad. Major General Layfette McLaws's 3,750 men held the center four miles with a mixture of Confederate and reserve regiments and 29

guns. Major General Ambrose R. Wright's 2,700 men and 32 pieces of artillery defended the left, a line extending to the Little Ogeechee River near the railroad crossing. This entire line was about ten miles along. In addition, the Confederates manned detached Fort McAllister on the Great Ogeechee River, as well as the batteries on the waterways east of the city.

Fort McAllister was isolated after Hardee was forced to abandon the outer defense line. McAllister kept Sherman from using the Great Ogeechee River as a link to the Federal navy and resupply. Resupply for Sherman meant not only provisions but heavy artillery and ammunition for a siege of Savannah. Hardee, without communication to McAllister, hoped it could hold out long enough for Sherman to be forced to move elsewhere to rendezvous with the Union navy.

Hardee ordered the Savannah River Squadron, which had been largely inactive since its 1862 activities in conjunction with Fort Pulaski, up the river to defend the Charleston and Savannah Railroad bridge, which was beyond the inner line of defenses. Commodore William W. Hunter sent his gunboats *Macon* and

Sampson, along with the tender *Resolute*, to protect the bridge.

On December 9 Confederate General Pierre G. T. Beauregard arrived in Savannah from Charleston. The Creole commanded the department in which Savannah was located. He urged Hardee to make arrangements to abandon the city if he could not successfully defend it. Hardee stated that he had no plans to evacuate Savannah but that if it became necessary, he planned to use the Savannah River gunboats to ferry his men to South Carolina. Beauregard suggested that Hardee construct a pontoon bridge, to which Hardee objected as a waste of labor and as an obstruction of the river.

On December 10 Hardee sent orders, by the *Ida*, for Hunter's squadron to burn the bridge. Federals had established batteries along the river and disabled the *Ida*, which had played a conspicuous role earlier in the war. Aground, she was captured and burned by Captain Henry A. Gildersleeve, of the 115th New York. On December 11, two companies of the 3d Wisconsin reached Argyle Island, between the railroad bridge and Hutchinson's Island. The next morning six more companies arrived. Reinforcements soon moved onto the northwestern tip of Hutchinson's Island. On December 12, Commodore Hunter's squadron, which had been guarding the railroad bridge, received orders to destroy it and return to Savannah. They burned the bridge, but as they returned to the

city, they encountered Federal forces who had prepared for the possibility. When the gunboats *Macon* and *Sampson* and tender *Resolute* approached, a Federal battery opened on them. As the *Resolute* turned, she hit the gunboats, lost control, and ran aground on Argyle Island, where she was immediately taken by men of the 3d Wisconsin. The two gunboats were able to escape the battery and continued up river to Augusta.

To the south on December 9 Confederate troops who had been guarding the approaches to Fort McAllister realized how badly they were outnumbered by the approaching Federals. They abandoned their position and moved south across the Altamaha River. McAllister's

garrison was now isolated on the south bank of the Great Ogeechee River. A month's provisions would enable the men to withstand the isolation. Great stocks of ammunition had been moved to the magazines. All of the trees within a half mile of the fort had been cut. The landward rear wall of the fort was strengthened and guns moved to cover this approach. "Ground torpedoes"—land mines— covered the land approaches.

The next day, December 10,

THE SAVANNAH RIVER SQUADRON SURROUNDS FEDERAL VESSELS IN NOVEMBER 1864.

(LC)

GEORGIA CIVILIANS DURING SHERMAN'S MARCH

As Union soldiers marched out of Atlanta on the morning of November 16, 1864, they anticipated following William Sherman's orders to "forage liberally on the country."

Martha Amanda Guillen measured the Federal advance that first day by observing smoke plumes on the horizon. Near Stone Mountain Thomas Maguire described the losses on his farm as the "destruction of Jerusalem on a small scale."

On November 17 the

PHOTOGRAPH OF WILLIAM T. SHERMAN AND FIVE OF HIS GENERALS TAKEN AFTER THE INFAMOUS MARCH TO THE SEA. L–R: O. O. HOWARD, JOHN A, LOGAN, W. B. HAZEN, SHERMAN, JEFFERSON C. DAVIS, AND H. W. SLOCUM.

(LC)

blue columns reached Dolly Sumner Lunt Burge's plantation near Covington.

"But like Demons they rushed in!" Burge wrote. "To my smoke-house, my Dairy, Pantry, Kitchen and Cellar, like famished wolves they come, breaking locks and whatever is in their way. The thousand pounds of meat in my smoke-house is gone in a twinkling, my flour, my meat, my lard, butter, eggs, pickles . . . are all gone. My eighteen fat turkeys, my hens, chickens and fowl, my young pigs are shot down

in my yard and hunted as if they were the rebels themselves."

At Chamblee's Mill an old blind mule pulling a wagon filled with six grieving women and the coffin of a small child to a cemetery was seized by soldiers. Foragers at Birdsville Plantation dug up the graves of twin infants, four days dead, while searching for treasure.

As a Spalding County farm was being sacked, a woman glanced out a window and noticed that it was snowing.

"No, misses," a servant replied. "Those men are ripping up all your feather beds and pillows to see the feathers fly."

Louise Caroline Reese Cornwell was forced to feed General O. O. Howard, one of Sherman's four corps commanders, at her home in Hillsboro. She found it strange that while Howard "sat at the table and asked God's blessing, the sky was red from flames of burning houses." General Howard himself would soon note "many instances of the most inexcusable and wanton acts."

The civilians reacted with bitter defiance. "Our men will fight you as long as they live," a woman said quietly as her farm was stripped of food, then she waved at her children and continued, "and these boys'll fight you when they grow up."

Sherman seemed unable to comprehend their hatred, writing to his wife, Ellen, "I doubt if history affords a parallel to the deep and bitter enmity of the women of the South. No one who sees them and hears them but must feel the intensity of their hate."

Sherman's army marched swiftly to Milledgeville, the midpoint of the journey, where they rested for several days. Although soldiers had destroyed considerable property and cleaned the country of provisions, they had molested few civilians. That changed after skeletal escapees from the infamous Andersonville prison camp reached Union lines.

In Irwinton on November 25 an officer wrote that "the boys had a good time last night. Wrecked town; recovered valuables." Next day the men were lined up and read an order prohibiting looting and arson for "I guess the twentieth time," he concluded.

As the march slowed from cold rain, swampy roads, and resistance, soldiers found time for mischief. Near Louisville a squad took Mrs. Nora M. Canning's elderly husband into a swamp to persuade him to divulge the location of his valuables, which were stored in a Macon bank. Rejecting this reply, the Federals tossed a rope over a branch and tied a noose around Canning's neck. The men trice hoisted Canning up until he was unconscious, then settled for his watch.

"Oh! the horrors of that night!" Mrs. Canning wrote of caring for her husband, who "lay with scorching fever, his tongue parched and swollen and his throat dry and sore. He begged for water and there was not a drop. The Yankees had cut all the well ropes and stolen the buckets."

At Magnolia Springs, near Millen, Sherman's troops burned an empty Confederate prison camp that dwarfed Andersonville. The primitive conditions of the camp "made my heart ache," declared Chaplain George Bradley, "miserable hovels barely fit for swine." Soldiers' hearts were

further hardened toward residents of the Confederacy. Learning that hounds were used to track escaped prisoners, they shot every dog they encountered, including a poodle. "There's no telling what it'll grow into if we leave it," a raider told its owner.

Federals overran Mrs. Charles Colcock Jones's plantation near Midway on December 15. She watched in horror as they seized ducks and chickens, "tearing them to pieces with their teeth like ravenous beasts."

One day later, Cornelia Screven prepared food for her children three times, only to have soldiers snatch it from their plates. She begged them to leave some for her hungry children, but a Federal snarled, "Damn you, I don't care if you all starve," a scene repeated across Georgia.

After capturing Savannah, Sherman estimated that his army had stolen 7,000 horses and mules, 20,000 head of cattle, 20 million pounds of corn and fodder, and an incalculable number of hogs, chickens, turkeys, vegetables, and fruit. Sherman believed his army had inflicted $1 billion worth of destruction on Georgia—$20 million military value—the remainder pure vandalism.

"This may seem a hard species of warfare," Sherman wrote, "but it brings the sad realities of war home to those who have been directly or indirectly instrumental in involving us in its attendant calamities." The modern term is total war, waged against combatants and civilians alike.

— *Jim Miles*

Sherman's forces moved on the Savannah defensive line. From right to left were the XVII, the XIV, and the XX Corps; the XV Corps was on the north side of the Great Ogeechee River. Light skirmishing occupied the Federals, but they made no effort to break Hardee's lines. Sherman did not press his assault but rather tried to establish contact with the navy off the coast.

On December 9 Sherman's men had built a pontoon bridge across the Ogeechee and on the tenth they rebuilt King's bridge, a major causeway across the Ogeecheee River about a mile above the destroyed railroad bridge. At the same time Sherman ordered Kilpatrick to his right; the cavalrymen reconnoitered the area around Fort McAllister on the twelfth

with the intention of taking the fort the next day. Confederate Major George W. Anderson and a small party of scouts collided with Kilpatrick's advance just south of King's bridge. In the brisk skirmish that ensued, the Confederates were able to withdraw into Fort McAllister. The troopers rode out to Genesis Point but stopped short of the causeway to the fort. Shortly thereafter a courier arrived with Sherman's revised orders to Kilpatrick, namely, that he not take the fort but turn the mission over to the infantry. Kilpatrick withdrew and set up his headquarters at Strathy Hall, home of Confederate Lieutenant Colonel Joseph L. McAllister, on whose land the fort had been built. Kilpatrick then sent the 9th Michigan Cavalry to take Kilkenny Bluff in anticipation of linking with the navy in Saint Catherines Sound. The remainder of the troopers spread out through the counties to the south, and some went to the site of Sunbury on the Midway River, a deepwater port abandoned from colonial times. Kilpatrick would make contact with the *Fernandina* on the thirteenth.

Sherman ordered Brigadier General William B. Hazen's Second Division of the XV Corps across the Ogeechee River to take the fort on the thirteenth. Sherman himself had commanded that division at

Shiloh and Vicksburg. At dawn on December 13, Hazen's 4,300 men crossed the bridge and moved east down the road on Bryan Neck to approach the fort from the rear. As his men assembled two miles from the fort, twelve scouts ran down the causeway a mile from the fort. They captured the unsuspecting Confederate pickets. The prisoners told the scouts about the "land torpedoes," both on the road ahead and outside the fort. The Federals forced the prisoners to locate and remove them from the causeway.

Removing the torpedoes took several hours and delayed the Federals from moving close enough to assault the fort. While Hazen was clearing the road of mines, he deployed sharpshooters to annoy the fort's garrison; artillery several miles upstream and across the river at Dr. Cheves's rice mill shelled the Confederates in McAllister. Because of the wooded and swampy terrain, it took all afternoon for Hazen to deploy his troops.

Hazen planned a three-pronged assault. Three regiments of each brigade

were set to assault the fort; the remainder were held in reserve. The 47th and 54th Ohio and 111th Illinois from the Second Brigade would attack on the left. The 19th and 48th Illinois and the 70th Ohio of the Third Brigade formed on the center. The 6th Missouri, 30th Ohio, and 116th Illinois from the First Brigade would move on the right. The infantry deployed in a line 600 feet from the fort on an arc from the river below the fort to the river above it. They were arranged "as thin as possible so that no man in the assault was struck till they came to close quarters."

At 4:45 P.M. they charged in unison. Slashed timber briefly impeded the men; they scrambled on and over the cheavaux-de-frise and abatis and swarmed over the parapet into the fort. Land mines outside the wall were responsible for most of the Federal casualties, "blowing many men to atoms." Within fifteen minutes Hazen's force had overwhelmed Major Anderson and his remaining garrison of 229 men and officers. In addition, 11 Confederates were killed and 21 wounded. Eleven heavy

THE STORMING OF FORT MCALLISTER BY GENERAL HAZEN'S DIVISION ON DECEMBER 13, 1864.

(HARPER'S WEEKLY)

guns, a 10-inch mortar, twelve field guns, 60 tons of ammunition, and a month's supply of food were captured. Hazen lost 24 killed and 110 wounded.

Sherman and Howard watched the assault from the roof of a shed at Dr. Cheves's rice mill, where a signal station had been built. As Hazen began his assault, signalers saw and signaled the Federal tug *Dandelion*. After the fort surrendered, Sherman and Howard went downriver in a skiff, had dinner with Hazen and the captured Major Anderson, and were taken to the tug, where Sherman wrote Stanton, Halleck, and Grant. He then returned to McAllister for the night.

Sherman was soon awakened and told that General Foster was aboard the

steamer *Nemaha* downstream. Sherman joined him and together they went to Wassaw Sound to meet with Admiral John A. Dahlgren aboard his flagship *Harvest Moon*. There, Sherman learned of the situation in South Carolina along the Charleston-Savannah Railroad. After arranging for supplies and the transfer of heavy siege guns from Port Royal to use against Savannah, Sherman returned to his troops.

With Fort McAllister in Federal hands, the Great Ogeechee River was open to the navy and resupply was at hand. A wharf and warehouses were soon built at King's bridge, the river cleared of obstructions, and by December 16 supplies were arriving and being transported to the army.

Federal action now shifted to the north. On December 16 Colonel Ezra A. Carman's brigade of the XX Corps crossed the channel between Argyle Island to South Carolina and established their position at Izard's Mill, six miles from Savannah. They could not move further down the left bank of the Savannah River because the rice fields had been flooded and behind them was a strong Confederate line. Sherman was reluctant to commit too many men to the left bank of the Savannah River since the Confederates had several gunboats in the river and could "destroy any pontoons laid down by us between Hutchinson's Island and the South Carolina shore, which would isolate any force sent over from that flank."

Carmen's move into South Carolina put Sherman's left within striking distance of Union Causeway, the sole line between Savannah and South Carolina. The road led to Hardeeville, where the railroad passed northward. As these maneuvers took place, Federal engineers opposite Hardee's inner line prepared sites for the now arriving siege guns and began to drain the flooded rice fields between the lines. Hardee, in turn, realized the danger to his only route of evacuation and had transferred Major General Joseph Wheeler's cavalry to block any Federal movement eastward toward the causeway.

On December 15 Colonel Orville E. Babcock, an aide of Lieutenant General Ulysses S. Grant, arrived with a letter from the commander of the Union armies, written December 6, informing his friend, "My idea now, then, is that you establish a base on the sea-coast, fortify and leave in it all your artillery and cavalry, and enough infantry to protect them. . . . With the balance of your command come here by water with all dispatch. Select yourself the officer to leave in command, but you I want in person." Sherman was furious; he had planned to move northward taking the war into the interior of the Carolinas. Fort McAllister offered an ideal site for the concentration and embarkation of his army, and Sherman ordered his chief engineer, Captain Orlando M. Poe, to begin the necessary preparations to develop the new port facility, should Savannah not fall.

With the fall of Fort McAllister, Hardee's position had become untenable. On December 17 Sherman sent Hardee a summons to surrender Savannah.

You have doubtless observed from your station at Rosedew that sea-going vessels now come through Ossabaw Sound and up Ogeechee to the rear of my army, giving me abundant supplies of all kinds, and more especially heavy ordnance necessary to the reduction of Savannah. I have already received guns that can cast heavy and destructive shot as far as the

A PHOTOGRAPH OF FORT McALLISTER TAKEN SHORTLY AFTER ITS SURRENDER.

(LC)

heart of your city; also, I have for some days held and controlled every avenue by which the people and garrison of Savannah can be supplied; and I am therefore justified in demanding the surrender of the city of Savannah and its dependent forts, and shall await a reasonable time your answer before opening with heavy ordnance. Should you entertain the proposition I am prepared to grant liberal terms to the inhabitants and garrison; but should I be forced to resort to assault, and the slower and surer process of starvation, I shall then feel justified in resorting to the harshest measures, and shall make little effort to restrain my army—burning to avenge a great national wrong they attach to Savannah and other large cities which have been so prominent in dragging our country into civil war.

Hardee promptly responded:

I have to acknowledge receipt of a communication from you of this date, in which you demand "the surrender of Savannah and its dependent forts," on the ground that you have "received guns that can cast heavy and destructive shot into the heart of the city," and for the further reason that you "have for some days held and controlled every avenue by which the

ONE OF THE CANNONS AT FORT MCALLISTER.

(LC)

people and garrison can be supplied." You add that should you be "forced to resort to assault, or to the slower and surer process of starvation, you will then feel justified in resorting to the harshest measures, and will make little effort to restrain your army" &c. The position of your forces, a half a mile beyond the outer line for the land defenses of Savannah, is, at the nearest point, at least four miles from the heart

of the city. That and the interior line are both intact. Your statement that you "have for some days held and controlled every avenue by which the people and garrison can be supplied" is incorrect. I am in free and constant communication with my department. Your demand for the surrender of Savannah and its dependent forts is refused. With respect to the threats conveyed in the closing paragraphs of your letter, of what may be expected in case your demand is not complied with, I have to say that I have hitherto conducted the military operations intrusted to my direction in strict accordance with the rules of civilized warfare, and I should deeply regret the adoption of any course by you that may force me to deviate from them in future.

Hardee, realizing his only course was retreat, began to prepare to evacuate his forces from Savannah. Using "rice-field flats," shallow skiffs 80 feet long collected from the plantations, he linked them as floats for a bridge from the foot of West Broad Street in the city to Hutchinson's Island to Pennyworth Island to the South Carolina shore. Railroad car wheels were used to anchor the flats in the river. Planks from waterfront buildings served as the bridging material; when completed, the bridge would be covered with rice straw to muffle the noise.

General Beauregard telegraphed Hardee on the seventeenth to speed the preparations for evacuation. The two generals agreed that the gunboat *Isonidiga* and armed tender *Firefly* would move to Augusta (they would be beached and burned during the evacuation), the iron-

clad *Georgia* whould be scuttled, and the ironclad *Savannah* would cover the evacuation. (The *Savannah*, unable to escape down the river, would be scuttled on December 21.)

The pontoon link to Hutchinson's Island was completed on the seventeenth; however, fog, ship traffic, and a shortage of rice flats delayed the construction of the remaining two sections until December 20. Wheeler, his cavalry reinforced with part of the Savannah garrison, held off Federal moves toward the causeway. The evacuation of the city, the eastern water batteries, and finally the lines facing Sherman was completed by 3:00 A.M. of December 21. Nine thousand soldiers, along with 49 field guns, had escaped. The mayor of Savannah, Richard D. Arnold, came out to surrender the city early on the morning of the twenty-first. At 6:00 A.M. Federal troops reached the City Exchange and raised the United States flag. Sherman was away conferring with General Foster and when he returned that night found himself in possession of the city. The following day, he sent President Lincoln word of his prize: "I beg to present you, as a

Christmas gift, the city of Savannah, with 150 heavy guns and plenty of ammunition, and also about 25,000 bales of cotton."

Sherman has been criticized for his desultory conduct before Savannah and for allowing Hardee to escape. Sherman feared that if his army was divided by the river, Hardee might crush the detached wing as Confederate gunboats, still active in the river, prevented additional troops from coming to their support. He realized that he needed to resupply his men from his new deepwater base. Finally, he had received a letter from Grant ordering him to send the bulk of his forces north on ships to take part in the final push against Lee; for this reason he had to keep his force intact and at the coast.

Sherman, along with Federal forces in Hilton Head, could have prevented Hardee's escape. Sherman was aware that the Confederates were building a pontoon bridge to South Carolina, yet upon his departure for Hilton Head Island on December 19, he left orders for his army not to attack the Savannah works until he had returned. Sherman's subordinates clearly observed the Confederate evacua-

tion on December 20 yet did nothing to interfere with it. Sherman's victory in Savannah was won through default, not brilliant tactical maneuver.

For his part, Hardee ably employed the limited tactical resources he had. He had 10,000 men, yet he had to secure the water approaches east of Savannah, as well as man the western defensive line. Hardee later reflected: "Tho' compelled to evacuate the city, there is no part of my military life to which I look back with so much satisfaction."

Between 1869 and 1872 Fort Pulaski's demilune was remodeled. Underground magazines and emplacements for heavy guns were added. Major renovations were planned for the fort; however, the project was abandoned when plans were developed to build

batteries on Tybee Island. After 1879 little further active military use was made of Fort Pulaski. During the Spanish-American War, a few men were garrisoned in the fort to man the guns installed on the demilune as well as at the battery on the north shore of Cockspur Island. Electric mines were strung across the mouth of the Savannah River and were controlled from Cockspur Island; the operators were also housed in the fort.

During the early years of the twentieth century, Fort Pulaski was totally abandoned. The moat again filled with silt and was overgrown with marsh grass. A jungle of brush and trees overgrew the parade. Snakes slithered everywhere. Although designated for inclusion as a national monument in 1915 under the American Antiquities Act,

THE OCCUPATION OF SAVANNAH

All through the night of December 20 Savannah's civilians listened with dread to the sounds of marching feet and cannon and wagons rumbling in the streets. The Confederate army was evacuating the city over a pontoon bridge and dawn would bring the Union army, which had burned its way across Georgia.

Confederate stragglers had plundered stores and warehouses in the night, and daylight found poor whites and slaves fighting over food stocks. Federal soldiers briefly renewed their looting activities until the arrival of General John Geary. The former San Francisco mayor posted guards and detailed a brigade to patrol the city. Sherman allowed few soldiers into the city, and those only by pass. Officers were required to remain in camp to keep their troops in rein.

Mayor Richard Arnold surrendered the city with a "respectful request" that its citizens, primarily women and children, be protected. The final Confederate edition of the *Savannah Republican* counseled "obedience and all proper respect" to the conquerers.

Sherman immediately pronounced military law superior to civil authority but stated that "peaceful inhabitants" should resume their "usual pursuits." Family, business, and social activities continued almost normally.

Sherman retained local officials to operate the city. Newspapers, "held to the strictist accountability," were regularly published.

Only 200 families refugeed from the city. The relatives of four Confederate generals who personally asked Sherman's protection were reassured that "no harm was designed" toward any resident.

Sherman later bragged that Savannah never had "a better government than during our stay." He remembered popular parades and concerts, teeming schools and churches, and plentiful provisions for all, rich and poor, black and white.

One Union soldier disagreed, describing the city as "a most miserable hole" with dilapidated buildings lining deserted streets strewn with dead horses.

The most disturbing reports were that Union soldiers desecrated cemetery vaults for thievery and shelter. "Surely such men are not human," declared Frances Thomas Howard.

Civilians were secure, although some ladies complained of petty theft and minor harassment. The women continually provoked much of that misconduct with their hauty attitudes. When asked by Charles Green, Sherman's host, if she wanted the general to be comfortable, a lady exclaimed, "No, indeed, I do not! I wish a thousand papers of pins were stuck in his bed and that he was strapped down on them."

Fanny Cohen, whose hatred for Federals rendered her "almost speechless," was forced to entertain an officer she later described as "a well bred dog."

When northern cities donated food to Savannah, Elizabeth Mackay Stiles wrote, "Then they think they are so liberal, giving us food, and they stole more from one plantation than the whole of New York subscribed."

During Christmas services civilians often walked out of church when Union chaplains participated. A Presbyterian minister declined the assistance of one Federal minister, explaining bitterly, "Sir, my people need comfort, and

that you cannot give."

Some gaiety was experienced during the holidays. As Union General O. O. Howard played with little Daisy Gordon (later Girl Scout founder Juliette Lowe), she noted that he was missing an arm. Told that rebels had shot it off, Daisy replied brightly, "Did they? Well, I shouldn't wonder if my Papa did it. He has shot lots of Yankees."

Whether they realized it or not, the people of Savannah were fortunate. Sherman's army had destroyed Atlanta and would soon torch Columbia, but in this beautiful city the dogs of war had been muzzled.

— *Jim Miles*

THE FEDERAL ARMY UNDER GENERAL SHERMAN ENTERS SAVANNAH ON DECEMBER 21, 1864.

(LC)

CIVILIANS ARE ISSUED PASSES BY GENERAL GEARY.

(FMTW)

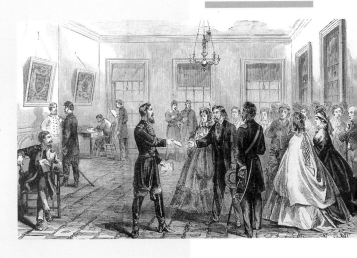

further action was delayed by American participation in the First World War. In 1918 district engineer Colonel John Millis recommended Pulaski's immediate preservation. His successor, Colonel F. W. Alstaetter, working with local Savannah groups, began to seek national monument status for the fort. Finally, in 1924, Congressman Charles G. Edwards introduced a bill to make Fort Pulaski a national monument; it was passed and on October 15, 1924, President Calvin Coolidge issued the proclamation. The site remained an overgrown jungle until the War Department transferred it to the Department of the Interior in 1933. The National Park Service then began to preserve the fort and develop the area for visitors. Blueprints, specifications, and other plans were available in the War Department files. Using funds provided by the Public Works Administration and labor

of the Civilian Conservation Corps, restoration was begun. Completed in 1938, Cockspur Island was joined to the mainland (McQueens Island) by a bridge across the south channel of the Savannah River.

Fort McAllister returned to forest and brush after the war. Henry Ford acquired the site with the tracts he purchased in Richmond Hill; he restored the fort in the late 1930s. In 1958, the International Paper Company purchased a parcel of land from the Ford estate and transferred the title to the state of Georgia. In ensuing years, the Georgia Historical Commission restored the parapets and bombproofs to their appearance during 1864. Parts of the *Rattlesnake*'s machinery have been salvaged and are also located at the site.